CALL FOR IIMS

TOPPERS INTERVIEWS

TRISHA CHATTERJEE

INTERVIEW OF CAT TOPPERS..

Somehow I wished to get into IIM C more than any other B school. Finally, I had the call of my dream B school. This was my first interview of the season so a lot of anxiety!

10th / 12th / btech : 93.07 / 80 / 76

CAT : 99.61 (overall)

VA / DILR / QA : 96.57 / 99.45 / 99.27

Category: EWS

Date: 26th Feb'2020.

Venue: The Orchid, Mumbai.

Panelist: 2 male & 1 female (Prof. Runa Sarkar). Let's say M1, M2, and Maam respectively.

M2 didn't utter a word for the entire duration. He was keenly listening & observing.

M1: Going through my documents he asked 'tell us something that you don't want us to ask you'

Maam: It's a tough one right? with a smile.

Me: Suprised at the question I smiled and started thinking. Meanwhile, M1 was flipping through the documents. I noticed him looking at my experience certificate as a faculty. Pointing towards the document I said "that one sir" and with a smile, he said "okay".

M1: Looking at my personal data form " so after Btech you worked at Pidilite post that you had your own QSR then a stint as a full-time faculty then as a part-time faculty... could you explain?".

(He seemed very confused or I would say unhappy and it was quite visible.)

Me: Tried to explain what I did and why. But he seemed unsatisfied.

M1: "Mere dimaak ka bharta ban gaya hai".

Me: I didn't knew how to respond but somehow the reflex action took over and with a wide smile I said "KUI SIR" ... yes in Hindi.

(Maam chipped in as a savior and explained duration wise what all I did. I saw she had noted everything on a piece of paper while I was explaining.)

M1: What is your view on the reservation being asked in Maharashtra? answer being specific to a state like Maharashtra.

(I didn't quite get why the question was asked. It was not a recent news at all.)

Me: Gave a diplomatic answer without picking a side.

M1: You speak like a consultant giving a bird eye view. take a side and give 3 reasons why so.

Me: sir its tough to take a side and I reiterated some of my earlier said points.

Maam: Ohh it was your birthday yesterday.

(Everyone wished a belated happy birthday. I said thanks and then continued.)

Maam: Okay, tell us about your QSR business experience.

Me: Told. But kept it short.

Maam: Right from the beginning. Who all were involved, logic behind location selection, product...... I mean everything.

(I was happy because now I was in my comfort zone. We discussed it for about 10 minutes. I would say I had a good conversation. Was happy for the moment until M1 chipped in.)

M1: Ankit would you answer my previous question. Take a side and give 3 points. Be specific to Maharashtra.

(Now I felt like running away. Truly speaking I was about to take a side but somehow maintained my neutral stand. Although this time I pitched in some numbers specific to Maharashtra and made my previous answer slightly number based.)

M1: Rehne do.

Maam: If given a chance would you like to change your decision of leaving Pidilite? why so?

Me: Yes definitely. Answered to why so in detail. Pitched in my why MBA in the same answer.

Maam: I see you have entered "n" in your personal data form where you had to mention your extracurricular activities. why so?

Me: (with all innocence look I could manage). Maam I found it confusing to put in certain school and college-level events with proper drop-down options for level of competition. So I entered all my extracurriculars in the next section which said "any other usefull information".

Maam: Looking at M1 and M2 "We should take note of that. It should be rectified in next year's form. Thanks, Ankit"

(I felt so relieved !!)

Maam: Given a situation wherein during MBA you have a good idea and a team. Would you choose to work on the idea.

Me: yes but this time I believe I'll take much more informed and calculated decision.

Maam: Vo keeda abhi tak hai matlab.

Me: Nodded with a yes.

Maam: I think we are done. Do you have any questions for us?

Me: (with a smile and humble tone) No ma'am but if I make it to Calcutta I'll ask questions in the classroom.

As I was leaving I was asked to have something. I picked a mentos (finally the fantasy of getting a toffee after C ka interview was complete).

Verdict: Converted!!!

Name-Ankit Mishra

Date - 22 Feb, 2018 (Morning Slot)

Venue - Indian Habitat Centre, New Delhi

Profile –

Xth -> 91.8% [CBSE]

XIIth -> 82.4% [CBSE]

B.Tech (Mechanical) -> 76.4% [Punjabi University, Patiala]

Work Ex -> 20 months at Infosys Ltd

CAT -> Overall – 99.81

VARC – 99.25

DILR – 99.86

QA – 97.75

General | Engineer | Male

WAT – "Vertical development of cities is better than the unorganized and

unstructured horizontal growth. What do you think?"

Hobbies –

1. 5-year Diploma in Tabla.

2. U-17 State level Basketball.

Pre-requisites –

1. This is the application photo that I uploaded for IIM C application, but I went clean shaved, of course. Thought it might become a conversation starter.

2. This is the diagram of a Tabla with description.

3. There were 3 panelists.

P1 is a male professor aged around 50.

P2 is a male professor aged around 35.

L1 is a lady professor aged around 40.

Interview –

Entered the interview room after a long wait of 4 hours. It was already afternoon by then.

A long walk to the chair.

Me - Good afternoon.

P2 - Please tell me you're not an engineer.

L1 - Please take your seat.

Me - (While sitting down) I am an engineer.

P2 - So Shantanu Waaaaali, konsi waali engineering ki hai aapne?

Me - Mechanical Engineering.

L1 - Why MBA?

Me – I want to learn about management as it interests me. *interrupted*

L1 - Why engineering then? You could have done BBA or B. Com for MBA.

Me - Explained how I was interested in engineering after school.

L1 - (Kept interrupting) So now you are not interested in engineering?

Me - Explained how I want to grow and develop myself.

L1 - Why not do M. Tech in your own field?

Me - Again explained why MBA while saying I want to develop myself.

L1 - What do you mean by develop yourself?

Me - There are a lot of things that I don't know about...*Interrupted*

L1 - Do you know about quantum theory? Spirituality?

Me - No

L1 - Why not learn about them and develop yourself in that field?

Me - I am interested in learning about management.

P2 - So you're a mechanical engineer.

P2 - What is Reynold's number?

Me – It is a constant. Can't recall.

P2 - What is Bernoulli's equation?

Me – It is related to kinetic and potential energy.

P2 – Everything in mechanical is related to those two.

P1 - You are very weak in academics.

Me - I have been working at Infosys since the past 20 months as an Oracle apps developer, that's why I am not able to recall.

P2 - So what do you do at work?

Me - I am an Oracle application developer.

P2 - Arre krte kya ho? Coding?

Me - Yes

P2 - Which language?

Me - PL/SQL.

P1 – What's the difference between PL/SQL and SQL?

Me - Told.

P1 - Still, why not only use SQL and save it in a file?

Me - Explained how it would be redundant.

P2 - Why are you smiling so much?

Me - I think it's because I am a little nervous.

P1 - Can we exchange 2 numbers without using a 3rd variable?

Me - No.

P1 - Are you sure? Your selection depends on it.

Me - Yes. (I was wrong . We can swap two variables without a third one.)

P2 - You don't look like the person in the application photograph. Draw your moustache.

Me - Drew it.

P2 drew a x-y plane, shaded 2 semi-circles over moustache, turned the page and asked me to tell which function has this graph.

Me - (After taking a good 20 seconds wrote) $|\sin x|$.

P2 - Beautiful.

Me – Smiling *A much needed boast of confidence*.

L1 - Why do you have so many C's in your grades?

P2 – The world is full of seas (C's). How many seas (C's) are there in the world?

Me - None, sir. Its spelled W-O-R-L-D. No C.

P2 - I didn't ask you to spell it *serious tone*. I meant SAMUNDAR.

Me - I'm sorry, I interpreted it differently.

P2 - How many seas are there in the world?

Me - I'm not sure, but there are 5 oceans.

P2 – What's the difference between a sea and an ocean?

Me - I'm not sure.

P2 - Which water is more viscous - sea water or ocean water?

Me - As I don't know the difference between sea and ocean, I won't be able to answer that.

P2 - Which is more viscous - sea water or mineral water?

Me - Sea water as it has salt.

P2 – What's the chemical formula of salt?

Me - Sodium.........*Forgot*

P1 - Graph ke time top par, ab fir se neeche..!?

Me - *Nervous smile*

L1 - So you have a diploma in Tabla. What's the difference between Kehrava and Teen taal.

Me – Teen taal is 16 matra and kehrava is 8 matra.

L1 - Play teen taal.

Me - It's better if I sing it as there is no Tabla here.

L1 - Okay.

Me - *Sings teen taal with all the hand movement and notations*

P2 bangs the table with my rhythm as I sing.

P2 – Okay. If I toss a coin from the Syahi of the tabla, what is the probability that it will land on the maidaan? *Refer the image above for meaning*

Me - Maidaan is the thinnest part of the Tabla so probability is very low. Also it depends on the size of the Tabla as they come in different sizes.

P2 - Do an analysis in 30 seconds and then leave.

Me - (After 10 secs) The coin will never completely land on maidaan as it is not thick enough.

P2 - *Interrupting me* Thank you. You may leave.

Me - Thank you (Smiling).

Verdict – CONVERTED !! :D

Name-Santanu Wali

First of all, it's gonna be a long tough waiting time till your interview starts (mine was serial no 8 so started 2 hours late)

2 panelist: P1 M and P2F

They gave me an extempore topic : Chipko Movement (speak for 1 min)

Then P2: what do you know about diode. Explain

Your fav subject.

About Fourier and Laplace Transform

Flipflops and where do we use them

About 2 theorem (I still don't remember what was the name)

Then P1: you have mentioned your hobbie as Badminton so tell me about players who have played badminton in olympics

Difference between Classical and Folk Dance and name 5 each

Difference between language and dialects

Sports and Education Minister of India

Name 5 minister from UP

The interviewers were quite rude and didn't appreciate the time to think for answers. Overall the entire conversation was based on GK around Rajasthan as if is my native town. My workex wasn't in conversation much and they grilled me quite about my hobbies.

But be ready for long waiting.

Name-Jaya Thadani

IIM Lucknow

Interview date-09/03/2019(afternoon Slot)

Venue- IIM Lucknow (Noida Campus), Delhi

My profile

10th-90.25%||12th-94.20||grad-83.9%(E.C.E fresher)

CAT Percentile-99.16

Wat topic- Politicians are not respected anymore

There are two panelists, a male in his 40's(M) and female in her 50's(F)

I am called in for the interview

I greet both M and F and they ask me to take my seat

F- Introduce yourself

A-told

F- What kind of books do you read?

A- Earlier I used to read a lot crime and mystery fiction. Lately I have also started reading a lot of historical fiction novels.

F- One book which had a great impact on you.

A- It was book theif. It just made me feel that war is not a solution to any problem. It just brings destruction and sorrow on both the sides. Peace is the ultimate solution

M- So, you are in the final year of your college. Is this your 1st interview?

A- No ma'm

F- How did you come here?

A- By flight

F- How many interviews have you given till now?

A- Ma'am (taking a moment to count), it's 5

F- Oh my God, 5 interviews. Ok, suppose you are my friend what advice will you give me if I am going in for my interview? Tell me 3 advices

A- Ma'am, first of all stay calm, don't get stressed. Secondly remain honest. In one of my other interviews they asked if I want to change my stance so that they could select me but I didn't. So, never lie. And finally brush up your academics

F-(laughing) So you are well prepared for your interview and you have brushed up your academics,there is nothing left for us to ask.

I get silent, don't know how to respond. Kept smiling

F- No no it's not like that. I am just kidding

Sigh of relief

M- So you are Electronics engineer, are you placed?

A- yes

M -Then why not work and then go for an MBA

A- told

F- you said in your introduction that you love making friends. How do you make one?

A- By talking to them on various topics and knowing about their like and dislikes

F-Ok make Sir your friend

A- Ok, so sir are you a professor here

M- yes

A- So do you belong from here or somewhere else?

M- No, I stay here

A- what do you do in your free time

M- I listen to music

A- what kind of music do you like?

F (interrupts)- Ok so now we are your friend. Do you think in an organization being over friendly is good or bad

A- Ma'am in a workplace being over friendly is not very acceptable. Friendship should be maintained but it shouldn't harm your work.

F- (enters into preach mode,gives me a 2 min lecture on how friendship can be harmful for an organization

I listen patiently

A- Sure ma'm, I will keep that in mind. This is also one of the reasons why I want to join MBA, so that I could learn proper behavior and tactics

Meanwhile M is smiling

F - Ok,. That will be all, here have something from the bowl(chocolate)

I took an eclair and thanked them

Verdict- Awaited. The interview was so casual, I really don't know how they we're going to judge. They didn't ask me any technical or gk question. All the time they were talking as if they are my acquaintance. Let's see what happens.

Name-Nivedita Singh

IIM ROHTAK Interview

23 February 2022 Afternoon session 1:30 PM

98.31%le (10/93.6/8.23)

OBC Category

Electrical Engineering Fresher from NIT Surat

Two male panelists both looked less than 30 years of age

P1 and P2

Duration:10 minutes approx Waiting time more than 3.5 hours

P1-Asked to show certificates.

P2- Extempore

Topic - Negative points of budget 2022.

P2- You were part of school cricket team tell me about that.

P2- What is GIFT city?

P2- Tell abt the social service group you are part of.

P2-What is capacitor?

P2- Why birds donot get shock when they sit on high tension wire?

P1- A question on probability.

(I don't know why but P1 started asking finance questions, I did not mention finance anywhere in my form)

P1- what is fiscal deficit and primary deficit? What is fiscal deficit of India?

P1- who is deputy governor of RBI ?

I said I only know the governor and he is Shaktikanta das.

(He said every one knows that ??)

P1- What is monetary policy and fiscal policy?

P1- How can RBI reduce inflation?

Said Thank you and asked to leave the meeting...

Name-Lucky Deshmukh

Date: 07 March, 2021

Venue: VCNow, Madhapur, Hyderabad

I reached at around 7:30AM. IIM Ahmedabad was the only IIM to conduct in-centre interviews this year. We were supposed to go to the centre, give our AWT and then attend our interview via video conference.

Post my Aadhaar verification, I was asked to sit in a room with 10 odd other aspirants. The AWT was supposed to begin at 8:00 AM. Other students from my panel were yet to come. Meanwhile I had memorized some names of the students in my panel from the Aadhaar verification process. So I spent the next 20 minutes analyzing their profiles on Linkedin (DO. NOT. DO. THIS. STUPIDITY.) I realized I was the only fresher there and got extremely intimidated.

Fun fact: 4 aspirants from my very panel got into IIMA. We just connected. ?

Now, it's about 7:55AM when a 45-ish professor enters the room and says something on the lines of, "Your AWT will begin in 5 mins. I will let you know when you'll have to put your phones aside. Put your phones on silent. Any sound will lead to your instant disqualification." Now, I thought I still have 5 minutes, let's fiddle around with some news.? All the other students from my panel had put their phone aside by now. That's when the professor comes inside, sees me with my phone and shouts, "WHAT DID I JUSSSTTT SAY..!!!! WHAT DID I JUST SAYY..!!!!" I immediately apologised and put my phone away. I was on the verge of crying but had to give my AWT. How could I mess my mindset up on the most important day of my life. I had worked hard for this day since the last 6 months relentlessly. How could I be so damn stupid. But once the AWT started, I got into the flow of it and came up with what I thought was a pretty beautiful answer. I was very satisfied with what I had written.

I was the 3rd in my panel. So, I spent the next 25 odd minutes, timing the students who went prior to me, judging their reactions with no conclusions whatsoever?.

And finally, my turn did come. I went in pretty calm. The setup was a conference room, where the student would be sitting at one end of a big round table and there will be two GIANT screens put up side-to-side on the other end, the left one had the interviewee and the right one had the interviewers.

My panel had 2 professors. P1 was a 50-ish male and P2 was a 35-ish female. Both were extremely welcoming and friendly. We exchanged usual pleasantries and began the interview.

P1: (I hadn't yet removed my mask, I had just taken my seat) It's absolutely your choice to keep or remove your mask. (I removed my mask).

P1: So, Bhavani or Susmitha?

Me: Anything will do, Sir.

P1: Ok, we'll call you Sushmita. So, Bhavani, Susmitha, what's the connection?

Me: (I gave the elaborate backstory behind my name which turned out to be a 1 minute monologue?. They heard it patiently. It ended on how Susmitha broken down is, Su-good and Smitha-smile.)

P2: Yes, you indeed have a good smile.

Me: Thank you, Mam.

P1: So, Sushmita, Why MBA?

Me: (I gave my well prepared answer. It included some personal reasons involving my father.)

P1: (countered my answers for a good 5 minutes.)

Me: (answered all of them pretty confidently. He seemed convinced at the end.)

P1: Sushmita, are you good in Maths?

Me: (didn't want to be grilled on the topic, so answered in the negative) I wouldn't say it's my strongest point, Sir. I used to be very good in Maths. In fact, it was Maths that I had scored the highest during my JEE. But, Engineering Maths has proved it otherwise.

P1: But you are an engineer, that too an IITian. How can you not be good in Maths..!!? You know that MBA does have a lot of Maths in it?

Me: (answered on the grounds that the Maths in MBA doesn't go beyond calculus and statistics. And how I knew of what I was signing up for.)

P1: (asks me few questions on Continuity, Differentiation, Limits and Quadratic Equations)

Me: (answered all of them)

P1: Do you follow politics?

Me: Not really, Sir.

P1: Can you make an educated guess and tell me which all states will be having their elections in the coming 2 months?

Me: (Luckily, I knew the answer to this question as I was well versed with the politics of all the states with an IIM because of preparing for their respective interviews.)

P1: Tell me the political parties prevalent in West Bengal.

Me: (answered with TMC, BJP and INC)

P1: Do you know the full form of TMC?

Me: (absolutely knew the answer, but my stupid brain blacked out for some inexplicable reason. I literally said, "Yes, Sir." and went silent. ??♀???♀???♀?
I asked for a moment, suddenly remembered and yelled, "Trinamool, YES, TRINAMOOL CONGRESS," like I was Archimedes from his Eureka moment.)

P1: (laughing at this point. THANKFULLY.) Can you tell us about the political scenario in West Bengal?

Me: (answered what I remembered from the preparation for IIM Calcutta interview (11 February, 2021) in a structural format.)

(P1 asked me some cross questions. I tried answering all of them. We were having a healthy conversation at this point. But I realised I couldn't afford to let my interview run in this direction since I didn't have a good knowledge in it and was running out of content from the interview I had prepared for, almost a month ago. Had it been Gujarat's politics, I could have answered so much better. So, I ultimately decided to be honest and resorted to the good old, "I am sorry, Sir. I do not have a good idea of this. I need to look into it.")

P1: Okay, no problem. Do you know the richest person today?

Me: Yes, Sir, last I checked it was Elon Musk.

P1: Are you sure? Is he the richest person today?

Me: I didn't check it today, Sir. I'm sorry I don't know.

P1: Make an educated guess.

Me: It must be Jeff Bezos, Sir. (It was. But I wanted to flaunt my knowledge of the top 10 richest people. So, I went ahead and named 5–6 other top richest people. ?)

P2: Yes, it is Jeff Bezos. Do you know Elon Musk?

Me: Yes, Mam.

P2: What's he in news for these days?

Me: (answered with the Bitcoin fiasco that was trending those days. Also with how his single tweet had caused Signal to boom.)

P2: So, he is not an MBA. And yet a CEO. He's recently said, "MBAs do nothing but work on spreadsheets." Do you agree with his statement?

Me: I absolutely do not. MBAs have so much more to do than that. Some of the world's leading CEOs today have an MBA degree. And even if they don't, they have a team of MBAs from reputed institutes. (Gave an example of how the successor of Amazon is an MBA. Told how Satya Nadella and Sundar Pichai are MBA too. And gave a list of about 5–7 other CEOs who were MBAs)

P1: Sundar Pichai is an IITian, no?

Me: Yes, Sir. But Satya Nadella and Sundar Pichai also have MBA degrees from Chicago Booth and Wharton respectively.

P1: (sounds surprised) So, tell me about your final year Project.

Me: (answers in detail)

P1: (asks for how it is relevant)

Me: (answers)

(P1 asks for few more technicalities. I answered all of them.)

P1: So, Sushmita, I can see an exponential growth in your undergraduate academics. We usually see most engineers, especially IITians, go through a decreasing curve. Can you tell me about it? (I had started with a 7.0 in first semester and ended at 9.6)

Me: (tells them about my journey.)

P1: good, good. We need academically oriented students here. So, are you placed currently?

Me: No, Sir. I didn't sit for placements as this was my primary focus. I didn't want to hog on another person's job.

P1: But, you do need to have a backup, no?

Me: Yes, Sir. My interviews end on April 2. My college conducts its placements till the end of May. I will seriously attend for my placements then. I have already dropped a year for JEE. I can not afford to lose another year. So, I will try seriously for a job and prepare for CAT again this year, in case things don't fare well. (I did eventually get decently placed in college.)

P1: (seems satisfied) asks if I have any questions.

I ask. P1 answers.

P1: Please take a toffee from the bowl.

I take a candy from the bowl and leave.

This is the toffee that I got and still have it safely stored with me. And will keep it for eternity?♥?

Overall, it was a pretty chill interview. Which had me even more nervous. Because I had seen several examples of terrible interviews getting converted and the smooth ones getting rejected.

Result: converted.

Edit 1:

Oh my god.!! 15 upvotes and 400+ views in 1 hour. Thank you so much?♥?

Edit 2:
134 upvotes..!!!! Thankkk youuuu..!!!! ?♥?

Edit 3:

269 upvotes..!!?♥? I just can't evennn..!!

Name-Bhavani Susmita

This was my only IIM interview till date. Applied for- IIM Udaipur

Interview lasted 10 minutes, it was a disaster. I was last in round for 10 candidates for online round. And it was expected that the panelist would be tired by this time. I am writing this experience here on quora right after my interview.
Panelist - One Male (M) and one female Professor (F)

Date : 25 Feb 2022
Mode : Online Zoom Meeting

Background-

GEM
10th - 10 CGPA
12th - 94%
CGPA - 6.96
Work Experience: 3 years
CAT score- 92.11 %ile (Yes I got the call because my 10th and 12th marks were relatively good ;) ,so combined PI score for round 1 was good.
(I scored 79.26 %ile in DI;LR thereby missing IIM Indore cutoff by 0.74 %ile cutoff wise)

Interviewer- Tell us about yourself

Me: I joined BTech 2013–17 for ECE in Punjab Engineering College. Couldn't get dream placement, prepared 1–1.5 years for Civil Services and other competitive exams but couldn't get through.

Then applied for Advance PG course for Diploma in Advanced Computing in CDAC ACTS in August 2018. Got placed in Nokia. Worked in Nokia for 2 years 7 months, I explained my role in an elaborated way .

Me:
Some hardcore techie stuff, but they weren't seemed interested.

Interviewer- Why your grades and CGPA in college very low?

Me: I said I got good grades in 10th and 12th because I worked consistently there but in college I tried working on last week of exam and could never able to get grades based on extempore preparation

Interviewer- But then you will again have to work hard in IIM and study, won't you fear you will again fail, working hard.

Me: Sir, this was in 2013–17 phase and now I have evolved much. At that time I wasn't sure should I be working in technical or Civil Services but yes after 4–5 years now, the picture seems quite perfect. I am now working in technical domain for 3 years and if you see my CDAC grades, there was a gradual improvement.

(Male Interviewer didn't seemed convinced. He was in a hurry to wrap things up)

Male Interviewer- Okay Rajeev, you tell us 3 good things about your hometown and 3 weaknesses.
Me: I belong to Amritsar. industry wise this isn't much suited for employment. Amritsar is mainly based on tourism. People from all over the world come and visit Kashmir + Amritsar circuit. Other good thing is the cuisines of Amritsar. There are certain hotspots which only a local person would know. So tourism wise, it is good.
Amritsar hasn't been able to produce much jobs so we see many youth going to abroad or Canada. One industry I see booming in Amritsar is the IELTS , GMAT coaching industry. Everyone here is looking to go abroad.

Industry wise - Punjab is mainly an agrarian economy. Punjab led the green revolution in 1966 for wheat procurement and hence called the wheat bowl of India, but ever since then it has always been labour intensive and not capital intensive. Now today in 2022 ,along with Punjab, Madhya Pradesh and Western UP is also leading producers of wheat. Punjab hasn't been able to keep its industry up to the 21st century mark. Partly the problem has been the political structure which is very much chaotic right now.

Interviewer: Can you explain us the 3 pros and cons of Farming in Punjab?
Me: The pros are with 3 farm laws - all farmers will come under government data and this sector would be more organised. If private sector comes in arrangement with the farmers, it would be good for any external shocks for contracts. Cons is that , private sector can use it for their benefit

The cons of the farm laws is that people aren't sure about its outcomes. There is an extensive network of APMC, Mandis which they fear will be removed.

M Interviewer- Farmers not rotating crops, and some cancer related problems in Bathinda, aren't these the problems? What are your views on it?

Me: Yes, agreed 100%. Ours is the only state where Electricity is given free to farmers for irrigation purposes, for vote banks and MSP will be gone is also a concern and our water table is also dropping. Substances like Mercury are added and hence its causing cancers, so yeah this is alarming.

Interviewer: So what are your achievements? Anything you have played, worked in NGO?

Me: Sir I like Chess very much.

Interviewer: No no, I mean any achievement you have got

Me: Sir ,I like to travel.

Interviewer: No Rajeev, you are not understanding the question. I am not asking about your hobbies, have you played anything like badminton, Tennis?

Me: Sir, I like to play Badminton, Tennis and played locally, but not for any tournaments. Didn't joined any NGO or any club

Interviewer: Okay Rajeev, many thanks for your time. We are done, do you want to ask anything?

(I was like WTF, only in 10 minutes, you are done already, i knew its gone and there's not much bragging now)
Me: No Sir, that's it from my side as well

Verdict: Expected to be Rejected, will edit only if something is positive

I would like to say- keep your calm, and do involve in any extra curricular activities also if possible. Also, they didn't asked anything related to my field which I worked for 3 years (cloud and Devops), all they were interested were in

1. low grades
2. any achievements which I got (which was nothing) and
3. I was subjective of my answers instead of objective which means they could have felt I have talked more about my opinion rather than the facts if I could introspect- My answers weren't that polished while delivering and other thing was him and me both were speaking at very brisk pace, so calming down a bit of nerves was lacking

(Do give as many interviews as you can, in this way you can judge yourself to the rest of the world. I was also selected for IIM Amritsar but skipped the interview, and this wasn't a good move)

Name-Rajeeb Mahajan

An excerpt from the IIM Kozhikode interview, back in 2016.

The interview was running pretty smooth, until one of the interviewers (P1) saw my CAT percentile (99.89), and nudged the other one (P2).

P1 clears the throat.

P1: You've such a high percentile. Why are you here? You will crack IIMA and ditch us.

Me: Sir, IIMK is one of the best IIM calls I have, and I value it like any other call.

P1: But definitely, not the best IIM call! Don't you lie to us!!

P2: So, you come from Bihar. What's your opinion about Lalu Prasad Yadav?

Me: Extremely corrupt politician, Sir.

P1: How can you be so sure?

Me: Sir, his evil smile reveals it all.

P1: Looks can be extremely deceiving, my dear friend!

Me: Exactly my point Sir! A high percentile may not always mean IIMA material.

Both the professors raise their eyebrows for a moment.

...and the interview continued with some more weird questions.

Final Verdict: Selected.

Name-Aakash Sinha

WARNING: Long answer

Common Admission Process - 9 IIMs, 2017

Date: 20 Feb 2017

Time: 8:30 AM

Venue: IIM Trichy, Chennai Centre

Background: Chemical Engineer from BITS. 2.5 years work ex in Pharmaceutical Manufacturing. CAT percentile - 98 | 10/12/Grad - 89/ 89/ 71

First day, first slot of Common Admission Process of 9 IIMs. So, I didn't have any pre-conceived notions about interviewers/ panel/ process etc. Later it turned out, I was the first candidate in my panel too.

Reached the centre at 8:00 AM. We were directed to sit in a classroom which was the waiting room for candidates. The centre was very neat and clean, with huge classrooms, which were well-lighted and carpeted. Also, it was my first visit to an IIM classroom. Infra - Thumbs up! (Not much to worry on this front if you are joining a new IIM, since by now most IIMs have their infra up and running.

After a little wait, an administrative officer directed us to move to another room for WAT.

We were asked to take out our interview form (previously submitted online) and submit it. An attendance sheet was passed for signature and candidates were asked to note their panel numbers and sequence and denote the panel number on the top right corner of the form. On checking, I saw that I was first in my panel. First day, First slot, First candidate! What are the chances?

I was little relieved as being the first candidate is always good - No prior benchmarks for the panel ;-) and my process would be over quick and I could go to office (Had already taken 2 leaves in the previous week for

IIFT and SPJIMR interviews) :-D

WAT

WAT evaluation sheets were passed and WAT Topic was announced. We were given 15 minutes to gather our thoughts and write. The topic for our slot was - The Delhi high court judgement on copyright infringement controversy between publishing companies and the photocopy shop in a certain university.

The topic was careful not to mention names of any stakeholders, however I remembered this case distinctly - I read Hindu every single day from May 2016 till the date of interview. I wrote my WAT from a stakeholder analysis point of view but fell short of time towards the end and concluded concisely. This could have been better, had I managed my time better. During submission I glanced at the sheets of other candidates and people had filled both side of the sheets completely. I wrote a page and a half keeping the word limit in mind. I quickly counted words in a random line and the number of lines - it came out to be 290 words (limit was 300). I felt I did above average in this round.

Then we were told that snacks and tea are arranged and candidates can refresh and get ready for the next round - PI. I had tea and couple of biscuits and met some people I knew from previous interviews. We discussed the Infosys CXOs wages controversy as we were expecting questions over it in PI. (You will meet many people again and again in different interviews, because people have similar calls at similar marks) We returned back to the waiting room and I was waiting for my name to be called.

PI

My name was called and I kept my phone in my bag (we were told that phones cannot be carried inside interview room even in switched off condition) and took out my file and went in.

I entered the room and there were 3 panelists.

Left - Lady, probably in her early 30s (Mostly a prof.) (L)

Centre - Gentleman, mid-30s (Prof or Alumni) (C)

Right - Gentleman, late 40s or 50s (Senior Prof) (R)

The room arrangement.

I entered and wished the panel Good Morning and stood next to the chair.

L - Please have a seat.

Me - Thank you, ma'am.

C - How are you Nikhil?

Me - Nerves took over ... Trying to get the words out ..... (I stammer when I get nervous)

C - I asked how are you Nikhil.

Me - Finally the words come out .... I'm good sir, a little nervous to be honest. (With a smile throughout)

All interviewers smiled too. (As they say a smile goes long way and it never hurts to smile; and the first 30 seconds are very important to set the course of the interview)

Also, hint:- A very cordial panel. (Yay!)

L - Are you a resident of Chennai?

Me - Ma'am, I have been working here for the past 2.5 years. I'm a permanent resident of Uttar Pradesh.

L - Okay.

C was going through my form when I was entering the room.

C - Nikhil, your graduation marks paint a very interesting picture. What happened in the first two years? (My yearly GPAs are 6, 6.55, 7.89 and 8.15)

Me - (I was expecting this question and had tried to come up with all sorts of excuses during my preparation, but was never convinced myself)... Sir, I come from a family where all the emphasis was laid on academics and I never really had a chance to explore any other arena such as sports, extra-curricular etc. After I came to college I had this new found freedom. I got into sports, club activities etc. Honestly, I missed some classes too. Soon I realised that this is not the reason I am here and my core chemical engineering courses are pending so not much is lost. I started to focus on academics and improved a lot. At a point, I was top 5 in some chemical courses in my class.

Contd. .. They were listening patiently ... Sir, it's a mistake I regret till date but I learnt the hard way and will never repeat it in my life. BITS has zero attendance system and trusts students to make their decisions. I'm glad that I learnt this lesson on my own rather than a college rule of minimum attendance.

L - But the 9 IIMs you are interviewing for, all have rules for attendance. How will you manage?

Me - Ma'am, I prepared for JEE in 11th and 12th standards with normal schooling. I used to attend a full day of school, then go for 4 hours of coaching classes on alternate days, study till 1 or 2 AM and then attend school at 7 in the morning each day. If I join any of the new IIMs, I will definitely be able to put that amount of effort again.

L looked convinced because she did not question back.

C - Looking in to the form... So, you are working in a Pharmaceutical company?

Me - Yes, sir.

C - What do you do in your role?

Me - I told my portfolios and what I do on a day-to-day basis.

C - So, you said statistical process control. Are you six sigma trained?

Me - No sir.

R - (All the while he was quiet and observing me. I made eye contact with him once or twice till then.) What is a process?

Me - Gave a crude definition ... in terms of input (material, conditions, people, energy) and output (product, different form of energy, service)

R - What is statistical process control?

Me - I had prepared this ... I explained in lay man terms.

R - Okay. What kind of tools do you use in Statistical Process Control?

Me - I told statistical tools with some examples and their use.

C - Explain control charts.

Me - I gave examples of p, np charts and their use in the parameters monitored.

C - What other type of charts are there?

Me - Sir, we use only these two charts so far as the project is still in implementation phase. Based on my research I know of R-chart as well but have never used it.

C - Explain R-chart.

Me - Sorry sir, I don't know.

C - If you don't know then do you think you will be able to implement this project?

Me - Sir, my role in the project is similar to that of a project manager. I'll put together a team of experts from each departments such as Production, Quality Assurance, Engineering, Quality Control etc. This team will also include personnel from Operational Excellence who are statisticians and more well versed with statistics.

C - But don't you think you should know? (contd from previous question)

Me - Sir, I completely agree with you. I'll learn more and more as we go deeper in this project.

C -Okay. Do these people report to you?

Me - No sir, these are people with 10–15 years of experience. I am too junior to have them report to me.

C - Okay. What is the one challenge which you face while working in such a team?

Me - I was not expecting a behavioural question at this point ... thought for 5 seconds .. Sir, the people I work with do not report to me and are senior to me. It is a challenge to extract work out of individuals who do not report to me. It is very important to understand their behaviours and working styles and mould myself according to that to accomplish the task at hand.

C - Okay, good.

L - Tell us more about the program you have undergone? (I was part of a rotational training program at my organisation)

Me - Explained the program structure... rotations to different functions.. how it helped me gain maximum exposure in a short period.

L - Nikhil, your work seems interesting. You underwent a program similar to young leaders program at other organisations. Why leave now? (In short - Why MBA?)

Me - Ma'am, everything indeed has been great, however my exposure is limited to pharmaceutical manufacturing and is very technical in nature. I am seldom able to relate my work directly to the bigger picture. I believe an MBA will give equip me with the right business skills and I'll be able to approach my work with a more holistic view. Also, after my MBA I wish to take up a larger role in this field in order to have more impact.

L - Okay.

L - What has been your biggest failure in life?

Me - Told about how I am blessed with a stammering problem and was rejected in the SSB for NDA - Indian Air Force, Flying entry, which was my dream job. I think I got a little teary eyed here.

R - Jumps in with academic related questions as soon as I finish, maybe to throw me off. So Nikhil, what is a function?

Me - I answered in terms of input and output.

R - What is a set?

Me - Startled ... Managed to say - Sir, set is a collection of elements, which may or may not have a relationship with each other. (I was startled not only because I never expected a basic question but also because I did not remember the exact definition for such a "basic question".)

R - Okay. Then define a function in terms of sets.

Me - I talked about, domain, co-domain and range and cited an example of how these work in a function using square root function.

L - Nikhil, what are the two learnings out of your 2.5 years of career so far?

Me - Talked about how working closely with senior leaders in the organisation has helped me develop my skills and humility from experts who have a lot of experience and yet, are so humble and always mentor me - being new.

L - Okay. What about your extra-curricular activities? What did you do in school and college?

Me - Told about my extra curricular activities.

L - So you took part in any competitions, won anything?

Me - Yes, ma'am ... I tried to show the certificates...

L - Just tell us in brief.

Me - Told.

R - You also mentioned that you were the school captain (head boy). What were your responsibilities as the school captain? What challenges you faced?

Me - I told the responsibilities of a head boy - commanding morning assembly, ensuring conduction of morning assembly - just check if the students who were presenting matters were ready or not.

R - In your answer you used a word "just". When you say "just" it does not mean it's a challenge. Did you face any real challenge?

Me - (I was cursing myself for using the word) Okay sir .... thought a bit .... Sir, on annual school day and sports day it was my responsibility to lead the parade. The parade had students from every grade from 12th to 1st. It was very challenging to get the 6–7 year old kids to understand the march rhythm so that the parade presentation would look good.

R looked satisfied.....

You will have some good days and some bad days during your MBA interviews and during your good days you will be able to recollect everything and come up with answers on the spot. On bad days, you won't and you'll come out of the interview room kicking yourself.

This supposedly was a good day and my mind was working. I have had bad days too but that's an answer to a different question.

C - Okay Nikhil, last question. Suppose if you get admission into an MBA course and your company is offering you the role of Executive Assistant to CEO. Which will you choose and why?

Me - Never expected this question ... Sir, Executive Assistant roles are of two types. One which is purely administrative and I don't see myself in that role. The second role is more involving and the Executive Assistant would help the CEO in devising the firm's strategy and managing a part of his work for him. This role would definitely help me get a good overview of the business and I would be networking with the leaders of the organisation but an MBA would equip me with the right skills and knowledge which will be more beneficial in the long run.

C - Smiling ... Okay, thank you Nikhil. We are done. Please tell XX (next candidate) to enter after 5 mins.

Me - Okay. Thank you sir.

Put the chair back in place .. left the room...

PI lasted 30–35 minutes at least.

Verdict: Result awaited.

This was the best panel so far, which seemed interested and posed question from all angles (work, academics, behaviour). I believe this is the difference between and IIMs and other institutes. Not that others aren't good, SPJIMR, IIFT too had good panels and a very good process. But this is one thing which is not under your control. The panel you have is what you get. Needless to say, go in with all your skills and knowledge.

Also, this was my best interview performance amongst all the 6 I have given so far. Whether I convert this call or not - is for later. But I was happy that I fared well and could answer most of the questions.

Presence of mind, preparation and a warm smile will go a long way in your interview. Be attentive, take cues from tone of question asked, expressions of the interviewer and answer honestly. You will sail through.

As for me, I will update the answer with the Verdict.

EDIT (26 May 2017)

Converted 8 out of 9 new IIMs and waitlisted at IIM Trichy in the first list.

Name-Nikhil Ojha

Date: 22nd Feb'22
Slot: 2:30PM (Had my college exam from 5 :p)
Venue: Online - MNIT Jaipur Hostel :p

Profile: B.Tech ECE Fresher. Acads 95/95/81.
P1, P2 50+, P3 30-35

Overall Experience: Was a wholesome interview covering every aspect and literally my best of the season. Liked the way they broke the ice and covered all things from there.

P3: So, as you've not graduated yet, how is it going? Are you in college, doing an intern or having exams? (Mine was a mix of all these)
Me: I'm currently in college hostel only. Interning at A and semester exams are ongoing.

So you gonna join A after your graduation?
Told him how it was an internship opportunity rather than a full time role.

Asked about placement scenario
I told about my college overall- how most of the students got placed and companies are visiting even now

He then asked about mine specifically - status & company
I told him the company I was placed (P)

Ok, so rather than joining P, you want to come here. Is it so? Why?
Told them I don't want to limit myself to a single domain, want to explore the opportunities and how MBA can help me in that.
One follow-up ques on the same (told)

P2: Since, you don't have work ex, I have to ask you ECE questions.
Around 10 min discussion on OSI model, 4G 5G, CSMA/cd, Fourier, fast-fourier

P3 asked me about a competition I mentioned in my SOP
I had my primary education in a Hindi Medium school by Vidya Bharti which is affiliated to RSS. So basically it was an annual inter school competition organised by Vidya Bharti. And in my 5th class, I went to finals of it. Told what was it about - Our history, values, culture, GK.

And then a 'discussion' went on importance of history
(And it made me forgot that it was an interview)

The exact question was:
Is it even important to read history when your work is not even a bit related to that say finance or IB
Some counter questions were there.

P2: My pastime
Me: geo-politics & cricket. Told him that I'm learning capitals of d/f countries.

P1,P2,P3 were simultaneously throwing question at this moment.
Asked 3 capitals instantly
Answered all. He commented that's some serious learning :p

No. of teams in ipl now: 10

Name of new teams: Gujarat Titans, Lucknow Super Giants

Best team in ipl (after auction): Told Lucknow.
Told him how Lucknow got a balanced team with destructive openers(plus left-right combination) and a pile of good all-rounders and then both spin & seam department.

Asked if I mean it or I just picked it from somewhere
Told them how I watched the auction live and analysed this myself.

P2 did a Bit of cross questioning on KL Rahul lol (if he's really worthy)
Mentioned his consistency as how he's among top3 run getters for 4 straight seasons. On if he's really destructive: I mentioned in Punjab he was alone scoring runs and there was no support from other end that's why his SR got affected but he's can score quick runs we'll see that. Also this year as a part of team with strong batting line-up like LSG, he'll get that liberty to play aggressively.

But he didn't stop :p
And asked me why I'm being a fan of him and ignoring the stats
After this, CAME THE BEST MOMENT
P1 said, "arey, use Karnataka ka sb kuch pasand hai" (he likes everything about Karnataka)
Brought an ear to ear smile on my face :p

So you play cricket in your college?
Me: Sir, I'm not a part of insitute's team but yes I play in the hostel often even in the corridors. Also I played cricket regularly back in hometown before coming here.

P3: Where's your hometown
Told it's a village so he asked 1 ques about district.
It's in Bharatpur district, so question was about Area of Keoladeo Ghana there.

Next 5-6 min on questions about my state
Governor, most illiterate districts, largest district, No. of Municipal Corporations, State symbols - animal, tree, bird, flower.
Rank engineering colleges in your state

P1 then asked me about my father's business

Asked if I had any question
Me: No.

Around 25–30min interview but very structured and in flow.
Was definitely a ever-cherishing experience.

Verdict: CONVERTED

P.S. My first answer here. So kindly ignore typos or similar things. Do upvote if you like it. Planning to share other experiences too. Thanks for reading. Have a great day!

Name-Samayak Jain

IIM C PI Experience

Date: 30.03.2022

Two Panelists, both male

I greeted both the panelists and asked them how they were doing, before they asked me.

P1

1. Introduce yourself (cut me in the middle of my intro)

2. Tell me more about your work experience

3. Questions related to the data I use at work

4. He pointed out the fact that I scored extremely well in my macro papers, and comparatively poor in my stats paper, asked me the reason for the same

5. (stats rapid fire, Literally) Give me a scenario when mode would be a better indicator than mean or median

6. Which is a better measure, mean or median. why. give examples. (I said Placement reports, then a full fledged discussion on the reports went on for 3-4 minutes)

7. What all factors would you look at in a college or its placement report to analyse if it's a good institution.

8. 1-2 Basic eco questions

P2:

1. Tell me more about your work ex, he said that he didn't understand what I had said before (cross questions on the same)

2. What is a cross functional team, give example, Use an educational institution and tell me where can I find cross functional teams

3. Stats Questions (Are Placement reports normally distributed? What is a normal distribution? Central Limit Theorem?

4. What kind of yoga are you into, tell me about different schools and forms of yoga? (couldn't answer properly, asked me to read more about it)

5. Which apps do you use for yoga, (and I could see that he checked those on his phone)

6. Mathematical graphs (log and exponential)

7. GK Questions, State with the longest Coastline in India (I said Gujarat, but he tried to make me reconsider my answer, i didn't, read this for my A's interview :D)

8. Number of States and UTs in India (asked me to reconsider my ans, but I was sure. Asked me some basic gk questions that I can't recall now)

P1

1. Anmol, I just have one more question for you, Do you think you're special? Why?

2. Favorite Poet

3. Favourite Sonnet (asked me to recall it, Recited Shakespeare's sonnet 138)

IIM-C converted on 04-05-2022

Name-Anmol

IIM-K Interview Experience

Graduation - IIT Kanpur (Chemical Engineering)

Work Ex - UnAcademy (Content Manager)

Date - 23 March 2022

Morning Slot

Time 10:50 AM

Waiting Time - 5 min

2 Penalists =, Both Male, Let's say M1 (30+), M2 (40+)

M1 started with a smile.

M1: So, How are you? What are you feeling right now?

M1: So, What are you doing nowadays?

M1: What is UnAcademy?

M1: What exactly do you do in UnAcademy? Tell me about your role?

M1: Tell me some significant steps or initiatives you take for the content and marketing part of your company?

(as I told them about my role)

M1: What is the future of the Ed-Tech sector?

M1: What can we do to improve the retention power of IIMK students? (We all laugh at this)

M1: Why do you have poor grades in your Undergradution?

(I told them about my English problem and told them how I work on this)

M1: Did you hear anything about the tata group, what they recently captured along with Air India?

(I said no, I don't have any idea)

M1: OK, Do you follow business news?

(I said yes)

M1: OK, Tell me any business news you read recently. (I told them about the 10-minute delivery thing of zomato).

M1: What are your concerns regarding the 10-minute delivery model?

(and then a lengthy discussion on that)

M2 started with a deadpan face.

M2: Why do you want to do an MBA after a chemical engineering degree from a reputed institute like IIT Kanpur?

M2: You said you are interested in Management. OK, then tell me about two management thinkers from India?

M2: Please solve a maths problem for me, "If you have two sets of dice, in the first set you have six dice, and in the second set you have 12 dice, then what's the probability of getting 1 six from the first set and two sixes from second, and which have higher probability and why".

(I said, can I take time, after 20 seconds, I said I could not solve it).

M2: If you could not solve it, why do you take so much time?

(I said, sir, I was figuring out the possibilities and understanding the question, but after analyzing, I found that I cannot solve it now, and I smiled).

M2: Tell me about the slope of the Supply Curve?

M2: What subject do you like in Chemical Engineering?

(I said thermodynamics)

M2: What is the zeroth law of thermodynamics, and why is it called as zeroth law explained in layman's terms?

M2: What is the third law of thermodynamics?

M2: What is a perfectly crystalline substance?

M2: Tell me about Entropy; explain to me and tell mathematically about it?

M2: OK, now I don't have any more questions.

M1: One last question from my side. Tell me from which section your company is earning a maximum profit?

M1: Now, You can log off.

I said thanks to both professors, then logged off.

(M1 was very chill and smiled after each response and did cross-questioning on each thing. M2 had a deadpan face in the entire interview and was more focused on academics)

Interview Time: 20–25 minutes.

Advice: Be ethical in your every answer.

Result: Converted in the first list.

Name-Yogeshwar Ken

IIM Calcutta 9th February 2022, 8 AM

Profile

10th : 10 CGPA

12th: 94.8

Undergrad: 8.1 in Chemical Engineering

CAT : 99.88

Panel: Two Males P1 and P2

Joined the meeting room, was 4th in line for the morning slot.

Me: Good morning Sir

P1: Good Morning, So Vinamra I see you are an energy associate at PwC . Can you explain to me what exactly you do?

Me: Gave brief description of department, clients and main type of projects including current project.

P2: So can you tell how to completely reduce emissions in an industry ?

Me: No

P1: What about Steel industry, is complete mitigation possible ?

Me: Explained how steel production involves reaction with coking coal that are essential to produce steel at this scale and how emissions in it cannot be mitigated completely.

P2: So how can you reduce emissions in the industry ?

Me: Explained how the coal in India is of poor quality. Several methods to purify and improve quality to reduce emissions while burning it. Use of appropriate temperature and feed controls to monitor oxidation of gasses. Proper installation of electrostatic precipitators and scrubbers to reduce emissions released to the atmosphere. Switching energy sources used for heating purposes from coal to natural gas or even renewable energy .

P2: Do you know statistics

Me: Sir only the basics

P2: What distributions do you know and which would be used in steel industry

Me: Continuous distribution and Normal distribution

P2: What parameters would you use in the steel industry to monitor emissions.

Me: Mean, Median and Peak emissions.

P2:Anything Else ?

Me: Standard Deviation

P2: What's that ?

Me: Explained with formula

P2: What's all this squared and then rooting in the formula doesn't it cancel each other out ?

Me: Explained

P2: Do you know any discrete distributions

Me: Sir I Cannot recall currently

P2: Have you heard of binomial distribution.

Me: Sir I have heard of it but i cannot recall specific details.

P2: No worries can you tell me 2 places in real life where you use derivatives

Me: Told about the speedometer. (Couldn't think of another)

P2: What about acceleration ?

Me: (Me thinking it would have been derivative to say both velocity and acceleration) Yes sir , Sorry it slipped my mind.

P2: No worries let me ask you a simple question on equations

P2: If there is a linear equation in one variable how many solutions would it have ?

Me: (Visibly Confused, thought it should be one only) Sir could you give me an example

P2: (starts laughing) That's what I want you to tell . How many solutions and examples of the same.

Me: Sir it should be 1 to the best of my knowledge

P2: Are you sure ?

Me: Yes Sir

P2: What about $X+|x|= 0$

Me: (Panicking) Sir 1 solution

P2: Which is ?

Me: 0

P2: What about -1

Me: ...... Yes sir

P2: So how many solutions

Me: Sir 2

P2: What about

Me:(Me cutting in) Sir infinite solutions all negative numbers.

P2: (Smiles) That's all from my side

P1: So Vinamra I'd like to ask you a few questions about your hobbies.

P1: You mentioned you enjoy cooking, particularly baking. Can you tell me the difference between yeast and baking soda?

Me: Explained how one is a biological process with yeast consuming sugar to grow and create alcohol and how baking soda reacts with acid to produce CO_2 to leaven dough. How baking soda provides bitter taste but yeast causes souring of dough.

P1: So what would happen if I switch the two

Me: Explained the types of dishes where both are used and how bhaturas or brownies would become sour and breads wouldn't be as soft and how gluten formation (panic addition) would be affected .

P1: Does yeast help in gluten formation ?

Me: (Hurriedly correcting) No sir it's the kneading which helps with gluten formation however most places where yeast is used we knead the dough .

P1: Alright . You have mentioned your other hobby as Air Crash Investigation. Can you explain what you mean by that?

Me: Explained how I'm fascinated by aviation and how I used to watch the show Air Crash Investigation and read case files online about different errors and how the industry improved upon them.

P1: Have you heard of the Boeing 787 Max

Me: Sir you mean 737 Max

P1: Yes Yes can you tell me something about

Me: Gave detailed explanation of its history and reasons to rushed development due to competition with Airbus and how it was designed.

P1: (Cutting in) So why did it crash

Me: Incorrect design. Plane was designed with systems taking control away from pilots.

P1: Are you sure? Was it design error or sensor error ?

Me: Design Error (Partially correct was both)

P1:Ok Vinamra that's all from my side too. Do you have any questions for us

Me: Asked question on courses on behavioral economics

P1: Explained . You can drop off now.

Me: Thank you Sir, Have a nice day

P1 and P2: You too Vinamra.

Logged Off

VERDICT: CONVERTED

To be honest I didn't think my interview went as well as I hoped it would but I kept smiling even when I messed up in between or couldn't answer a few questions. However professors were extremely kind and encouraging and seemed genuinely interested in the conversation.

Name-Vinamra Aggrawal

The IIM Ahmedabad Interview : Season 1

It was a dream, and it still feels like one.

CAT 2013 Aggregate 99.99 | Verbal: 100.00 | Quant: 99.44
Profile: X ICSE 2008 (95.00) | XII Maharashtra Board HSC (Science) 2010 (84.7) | BTech Engineering Physics IIT Bombay 2014 (85.4) | Work-Ex:0

Extra-curricular: National Business Plan Competition winner, Startup core team Member, Institute Literary Arts Secretary with Organisational Color, National Level Quiz winner, International Quiz participant, Case Competition national runner up.

Venue: The Orchid, Mumbai
Date : 10.02.2014

PI:
Panel Members: One young gentleman (P1) and another older gentleman (P2) . The young gentleman was on the left and I think he was an alumni of IIT Bombay (he knew about where the lake was etc.).

Walk in, P2 is at the door and takes me inside. I take my seat, I was quite peaceful, had chit chatted with them a little bit before the PI. I was the first person of my panel (and I think the first person to be interviewed by IIM Ahmedabad)

Episode 1: The one with Pleasantries

P1 : So you seem to have run out of space for the essay on your teacher, do you want to add something else?
It looks like you ran out of space
Me : No, I just overshot a bit, I don't have anything to add.
P1 : Are you sure?
Me : Yes.

P1 rummaging through my file. I see he needs help.
Me : Can I take out my certificates.

P1 : Please do so

I take out my certificate along with the magazine made by our startup, and give it to them

Episode 2 : The WAT SWOT analysis

P2 : How do you think you did on them? Do you want to discuss something more, or should we move on?

Me : No sir, I think I wrote decently well enough

P2 : Okay, so do you know anything about such problems (with reference to the case) in present day India?

Me : No, I can't think of any. But I am aware of this one. (Pause, so I continue). There was this issue concerning Vedanta (wasn't there in the case) trying to get a captive bauxite mine.

P2 : So where was this?

Me : It was in Odisha, and the tribals opposed the move. It was given as a verbal confirmation by the government, and Vedanta invested a lot of money in it. But this issue cropped up and the tribals the MoEF opposed it, so it was disallowed

Episode 3: The one about Home 1.0 and 2.0

P1 : Okay, so you're from IIT Bombay, what is your favorite place?

Me : Lakeside (Powai Lake) and Hillside (Sameer Hill)

P1 : Which lake Powai or Vihar?

Me : Powai Lake

P1 : Why not Vihar? You're in which hostel?

Me: Hostel 4

P1 : So isn't there a road near Hostel 4 to Vihar Lake (Here is where I guessed he is an alum)

Me: Yes, but it's restricted now

P1 : Hmm, so where do you get potable water from in IIT?

Me: There is pipeline that passes by my hostel, I am not sure if it carries potable water from Vihar

P1 : Hmm, so how does Mumbai get potable water? What are the other lakes?

Me : I know of these two and Vasai Lake (which is tiny, couldn't think of anything else)

P1 : Okay, so you're from Pune, where does Pune get its water from?

Me : (Damn!) There is water carried by tankers from the Mulshi Dam area

P1 : So what about Khadakvasla?

Me : (Using sense to come up with something which couldn't be verified) My area gets it from Mulshi, the other area of the city gets it from Khadakvasla. (Which is sort of true)

P1 : Okay, so you stay in Viman Nagar, what are the landmarks there?

Me : Sir, there are a lot of hotels that have come up recently, it's become like a hotel road. Malls, and the air force base

Episode 4: The one with the Case

P1 : Okay, so you join IIM A and want to get in to hospitality, what are the parameters that you will use to judge a restaurant? (Placements case prep FTW!)

Me : (using paper) Footfall (Was going to add more stuff)

P1 : Okay, tell me about hotels

Me : Sir, occupancy in peak season and off season, the number of professional engagements like this one organized by IIM A (chuckle in the head)

Episode 5: The one with Physics, Chemistry and a TV

P2 : (Interrupts) Okay. So you talk about your chemistry teacher who had an impression on you. Why the change from Physics to Chemistry?
Me : I did both Chemistry and Physics for JEE
P2 : Right, right. But you chose Physics right, what was the reason?
Me : Nowadays Physics has become the node of major understanding of a sciences. Even Chemistry has become more of Physics and more of Chemistry. I was seeing this interview with the Bharat Ratna CNR Rao on Walk the Talk with Shekhar Gupta. Shekhar Gupta enters this lab and says "where are the Bunsen burners?" and CNR Rao says that we now do more of Physics, Quantum Physics and Schrodinger's equation. So, Chemistry has become more about manipulation of molecules understanding their effects on a quantum level and so on and so forth
P1: Hmm. So I am layman who thinks Physics and Chemistry are different. Can you give me an example of where they are being used together?
Me: Sir, Semiconductors. We understand the behavior of the matter using the Physics, Quantum Physics etc. and choose between various elements depending on the properties of the two.
P1 : You seem to be forcing physical and chemical properties against each other, aren't you?
Me : No. Physics is the understanding of the behavior of the matter while chemistry is the macroscopic manifestation of this behavior (I have no idea how I came up with this!)

Episode 6: The one with the shot in the dark

P1 and P2 look at each other
P1 : Hmm, okay. So can you give me an example of materials used in Semiconductors?
Me : Silicon, Germaninum Arsenic.
P1 : So any new elements or materials?
Me : (Thinking) Some variant using Carbon, I can't exactly recall. Graphene! (Phew!)
P1 : Hmm, so can you tell me a semiconductor manufacturing company in India?
Me : (Dafuq!) Texas Instruments?
P1 : But don't they have only an R&D lab in Bangalore?
Me : (No idea if the manufacturing facility is there) I think it is there
P1 : A pilot facility of some sort?
Me : Yes I think so (No clue!)
P1 : What are the other manufacturing facilities of Texas Instruments?
Me : Sir, the US
P1 : What about Taiwan?
Me : (Facepalm) Yes, yes Taiwan also

Episode 7: The one where you are on a TV Show in a TV Show

P1: So what is this Brain World Cup that you participated in? Is it something like the Olympics? I haven't heard of it, it should be quite popular shouldn't it?
Me: Yes it is. Very popular in Japan, but not telecast worldwide. It is a quiz competition that is held inter varsity with participants from Harvard Oxford Stanford etc. It was actually televised before the Olympic games in Japan.

Episode 8: The one with Gravitas

P1 : Hmm, so where did you do your internship?
Me : Sir I was working on developing an equity portfolio allocator at Gravitas, as a risk analyst intern. Gravitas is a risk management and technological co sourcing firm.
P1 : What was the goal of your internship?
Me: My project leader asked me to develop a tool that was targeted at retail investors. So I had to make a tool that was cost effective. I used global data sources such as Yahoo instead of Bloomberg which is a paid data source. Using this I made a tool with a simple intuitive interface coded in VBA with Excel as a front end.
P1 : Okay, so if you had to choose between hedge fund management and this economic policy outlined in the essay, what would you choose?

Episode 9: The one with Strategic Importance

Me : Sir, firstly I have an inclination towards strategy management consulting and I would like to work there and not a hedge fund
P2 : (I guess I wasn't clear enough) What does strategy management consulting have to do with this?
Me: I was saying that I would choose strategy management consulting over the hedge fund and it would be a choice between this and the economic policy. I have got placed at Monitor Deloitte, which is a strategy management consulting firm.

Episode 10: The one with the Masquerading Policy Maker

P1: Okay, so elaborate
Me : I think the environment is very important to us, and so is this policy. I have a few friends working on Energy policy making, so I have had discussions with them. The environment is something that will influence our lives (realizing that I am going too much on the environment thing). Parallely, the economy is also important to drive growth for the country. If we need to progress we need to push our facilities and drive growth for more prosperity
P1 : Hmm, go on
Me: Sir, I think we need to strike a balance between the two through good legislature and policies that are inclusive. (Back to my environment crap) I think when they say they are saving the earth and saving the world, I think it is more about saving humanity. We as a race are the most affected by environmental changes, and not the earth, which has been through great variations. For example, if we see Shanghai, life has become miserable because of the smog. We must progress along with taking care of how the environment is affected. This will only be possible with a strong policy that takes care of various parameters, sustainably.

Episode 11: The one with the Improvized Definition

P2: Okay, so you talked about Strategy Management Consulting. What is it?
Me: Strategy Management Consulting is the process of providing advice to clients to improve efficiency or performance, taking into account various parameters that are important and defined by them
P1 is looking through the startup's magazine in the meanwhile. He looked quite interested!
P2: Okay, so what is strategy in simple terms?
Me: Sir, it is the path that you design and follow to reach a certain goal

Episode 12: The one with Einstein as a Consultant

P2: So what is the application of Engineering Physics to Strategy Management Consulting? You seem to be switching again here?

Me: I actually I learnt a lot. I learnt how to communicate complex ideas in a simple manner. Can I show you an example on paper?
P2: Sure

Me: Sir, so in General Theory of Relativity we understood how masses behave at high velocities in the presence of an acceleration or gravitational force. Writing the equation of tensors is quite complex. But this idea can be explained in a simpler manner using the space time fabric and that masses create curvatures in this space time fabric, just like balls on a table cloth. We can understand how light bends, or objects behave quite easily using this. A black hole is like a hole through the cloth, more massive objects create more curvature
P2: Hmm, okay (He nodded his head quite a lot during this)

Episode 13: The one with Drive and Motivation

P2: So in your form you write that you worked where you learnt team spirit and drive and motivation. Can they co exist? Aren't they contrarian?
Me: I think team spirit is the framework through which a group of individuals synergize and work to use the power of a multiplying force. Drive and motivation is on an individual level, where each individual is driven or motivated to succeed. A team which has team spirit running through it, along with very driven and motivated individuals in superb.

Episode 14: The one with the elusive Toffee

P1 and P2 look at each other (Bakre ko jaane de?)
P1: So, nice talking to you. Here, have a toffee.
I grasp it say my thank you
P1: How did you rate the interview?
Me: I think it was good
P1 and P2 smile: Okay, you can leave
Me: Should I call the next person in?
P1 : No it's fine.

Really nice interview. Left me with a great feeling. It was really nice talking to such learned and well aware people!

Episode 15 : The Flashback

Both gentlemen take my courses in Operations and Finance (and I do like the courses too, deja vu) on campus.

Name-Aviral Bhatnagar

Profile: 99.6 percentile, 9/9/8. GEM with 2 years workex in Energy Markets.

IIM Lucknow:

1 Male Prof (P1) and 1 Female Prof(P2)

P1: Introduce yourself.

Me: Started with the intro - got cut short in between.

P1: Tell me the meaning of your name?

Me: Told. (I was about to relate my experiences with my name and its meaning at the end of my intro, but was cut short earlier)

P1: Why do you want to do an MBA? You have a lot of experience in robotics and energy markets already, why not pursue them further?

Me: Tried explaining. (he seemed unsatisfied - and was visible and vocal about it. I had to re-think my why mba answer after this interview.)

P1: Do you think India will be able to meet its renewable energy targets?

Me: Told. (Knew the market/policies inside-out and gave a good answer. In fact, reframed the question a little to touch upon the more important aspect of sustenance at high levels of renewable integration. I could see he was impressed but again cut me short in between)

P1: Okay, so you are from Lucknow. Who do you think is going to win?

Me: Talked about UP Politics for a while. (This was my strong suit and I had no hiccups in striking a casual and well-informed conversation on politics. Tried answering this with a perspective of my own - rather than throwing numbers and facts on the table)

P1: How many seats are there in UP?

Me: Told. (Answered some rapid fire follow ups as well - why RaGa is still in Parliament if he lost from his constituency, What about Modi ji's seats and the win count, How many prime ministers are from UP?)

P1: What other calls do you have?

Me: Told. (All calls apart from IIM C)

P1: Okay, we are done. Thank you. You may log - off.

P2 who had not asked anything till now (was snacking earlier) - jumped in at the last moment to wish me good luck :)

......

A short interview indeed. A lot of IIM L's interview experiences were short this year. First impression is going to be really important in such interviews.

Also, IIM L is the only IIM (afaik) where the CAT percentile and the past acads of a candidate are visible to the interviewer. You might also want to prepare for answers like - "why is your percentile so less in xyz section?"

.....

Verdict: Converted.

Name-Vishad Mishra

Contents